SEPTEMBER 11, 2001

Essential Events

SEPTEMBER 11, 2001

BY HELGA SCHIER

Content Consultant
Erica De Bruin
Research Associate, U.S. Foreign Policy,
Council on Foreign Relations

ABDO
Publishing Company

CREDITS

Published by ABDO Publishing Company, 4940 Viking Drive, Edina, Minnesota 55435. Copyright © 2008 by Abdo Consulting Group, Inc. Intenational copyrights reserved in all countries. No part of this book may be reproduced in any form without written permission from the publisher. The Essential Library™ is a trademark and logo of ABDO Publishing Company.
Printed in the United States.

Editor: Jill Sherman
Cover Design: Becky Daum
Interior Design: Lindaanne Donohoe

Library of Congress Cataloging-in-Publication Data
Schier, Helga.
  September 11, 2001 / Helga Schier.
     p. cm.—(Essential events)
  Includes bibliographical references and index.
  ISBN 978-1-59928-855-0
  1. September 11 Terrorist Attacks, 2001. 2. Terrorism—United States. I. Title. II. Title: September eleventh, two thousand one.

HV6432.7.S296 2008
973.931—dc22

                                        2007012006

TABLE OF CONTENTS

*Two airliners were flown into the World Trade Center
on September 11, 2001.*

102 MINUTES OF TERROR

At 7:59 a.m. on Tuesday, September 11, 2001, American Airlines (AA) flight 11 departed Boston, Massachusetts, bound for Los Angeles, California. Approximately 15 minutes later Mohammad Atta's voice came over the plane's loud speaker system. He announced to the passengers and crew that he and his companions had taken over some planes, were returning to the airport, and that everyone was to remain calm. A flight attendant quickly alerted American Airlines that their plane had been hijacked. Airline officials immediately notified the Federal Aviation Administration (FAA).

"A great people has been moved to defend a great nation. Terrorist attacks can shake the foundations of our biggest buildings, but they cannot touch the foundation of America. These acts shattered steel, but they cannot dent the steel of American resolve."[1]

—*George W. Bush*

Just minutes apart, at 8:14 a.m., United Airlines (UA) flight 175 left Boston for Los Angeles, and at 8:20 a.m., American Airlines flight 77 departed Washington (D.C.) Dulles Airport, also bound for Los Angeles. At 8:28 a.m., the FAA Boston Center alerted the command center in Virginia that AA flight 11 had been hijacked and was headed for New York City. They were asking for assistance, but it was too late. At 8:42 a.m., UA flight 93 departed Newark International Airport bound for San Francisco, California.

The events of September 11 would inevitably unfold. What was about to happen was so unfathomable that nobody could have imagined it.

The Attack

At 8:46 a.m., AA flight 11 slammed into the north tower of the World Trade Center in New York City. The impact, at 470 miles per hour (756 km/h), ignited tons of jet fuel. It turned the commercial airliner into a bomb powerful enough to blow a huge hole into the tower between floors 94 and 98. Dark smoke billowed into the clear blue sky on this September morning, and debris fell to the ground. New York City Mayor Rudolph Giuliani, New York Governor George Pataki, and President George W. Bush were

---

The World Trade Center

The World Trade Center (WTC) was comprised of seven buildings, the most prominent being the 110-story Twin Towers. It was originally conceived by David Rockefeller, a prominent American banker. Construction began in August 1966 and was completed in April 1973. The north tower was 1,368 feet (417 m) high, 6 feet (2 m) higher than the south tower, which stood 1,362 feet (415 m) tall. Surpassing the Empire State Building, the twin towers were the tallest buildings in the world, until the Sears Tower in Chicago surpassed them in 1974 at 1,454 feet (433 m). The towers filled the New York skyline. They were seen as a symbol of American economic power and strength, as well as of American diversity. The World Trade Center housed international businesses, employing citizens from nations all over the world. On September 11, 2001, all seven buildings at the World Trade Center complex were destroyed. The towers suffered direct hits by two aircraft. The building at Three WTC, The Marriott Hotel, was crushed when the towers collapsed. Another building, Seven WTC, collapsed later that day due to severe fire damage. Three other buildings were damaged beyond repair and had to be destroyed.

informed immediately. Firefighters rushed to the scene. Police helicopters circled Manhattan. The media arrived as well, bringing with them the cameras that would cover the event worldwide.

Inside the burning tower, people called their loved ones. No one knew just what had happened. Perhaps a bomb similar to the one that had hit the World Trade Center in 1993 was responsible for the towering inferno. Or maybe, just maybe, this was a terrible accident.

Hijackers

There were 19 hijackers who boarded the four planes. The plan had most likely included another hijacker. This position may have been intended for Ramzi Bionashib, a member of the so-called Hamburg cell of al-Qaeda. Bionashib did not get a visa to enter the United States.

UA flight 175 struck the south tower of the World Trade Center as millions of viewers were watching on live television at 9:03 a.m. The plane blasted a hole into floors 78 through 84. This was no accident. This was deliberate. But what, exactly, was it? An act of war? Terrorism? And where would they strike next?

At 9:37 a.m., AA flight 77 slammed into the Pentagon, the U.S. military command center in Arlington, Virginia, just outside Washington, D.C.

The Pentagon was evacuated immediately. The White House was evacuated. The Capitol was evacuated.

President Bush had been reading to elementary school children in Saratoga, Florida. He was whisked away on Air Force One to an undisclosed location, for fear that he might be a target as well. The FAA shut down U.S. airspace and ordered all airborne aircraft to land at the nearest airport as soon as possible. Air Force One and military jets circling Manhattan and Washington, D.C., were the only aircraft allowed to fly. Incoming international flights were ordered to return to their airport of origin or to reroute to Canada.

UA flight 93 ignored all orders. At 10:03 a.m., UA flight 93 crashed near Shanksville, Pennsylvania, following a passenger revolt against the hijackers. The plane had probably been headed for the White House or the U.S. Capitol. Death was instant for the passengers and crew on all four planes and for hundreds at the points of impact as well. Those left inside the Pentagon and the World Trade Center tried to get out as quickly as possible. Thankfully, many did.

Hundreds of people walked down the seemingly endless stairs of the twin towers. Escape was quicker and easier from the lower floors. The smoke got thicker and the heat more intense with every flight of stairs firefighters climbed in their efforts to assist those trapped inside. A few people even escaped the south

New York City firefighter Mike Kehoe helps evacuate people from the World Trade Center on September 11, 2001. Kehoe escaped before the towers collapsed.

tower from above the point of impact via the one stairwell that had been left intact.

THE TOWERS COLLAPSE

At 10:05 a.m., all hope of escape from the south tower evaporated in an instant. Two World Trade

Stock Exchange Closed

The New York Stock Exchange, the American Stock Exchange, and NASDAQ never opened on September 11, 2001. They remained closed until September 17, 2001. This was the longest closure since the depression in the 1920s. When the stock markets reopened on September 17, 2001, the Dow Jones Index had fallen by 684 points, the biggest one-day decline in its history.

Center collapsed floor by floor, plummeting into the streets below and covering Lower Manhattan in a cloud of dust and debris.

Inside the north tower, people were still struggling to escape. They were walking down the stairs with amazing calm and orderliness, many unaware that the south tower had fallen. Those stuck above the point of impact, however, had nowhere to go. The plane had sliced through all of the stairwells, trapping people high above the ground. Some jumped out the windows, trying to escape the smoke and the heat the only way they had left, meeting certain death on the pavement below. Others called their loved ones to say good-bye.

Then, at 10:29 a.m., all calls from the north tower went dead. One World Trade Center collapsed.

Lives Lost

In just 102 minutes, 2,973 people died—onboard the four hijacked aircraft, in and around the twin towers, and at the Pentagon. Among the dead were 343

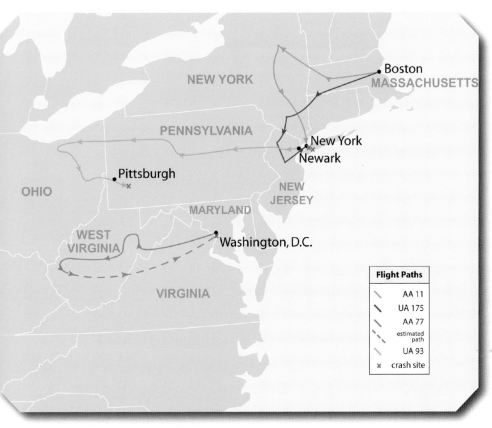

Map of the terrorist routes on September 11, 2001

New York firefighters and paramedics, 23 police officers, 37 Port Authority police officers, and 19 hijackers.

They were mothers, fathers, sons, daughters, brothers, sisters, friends, and loved ones. They were old and young, rich and poor. They were black, white, Hispanic, Asian, German, French, Japanese,

Australian, Christian, Jewish, Muslim, and Buddhist. They were flight attendants, police officers, traders, producers, tourists, waiters, lawyers, firefighters, and priests.

They were people—real people. When they woke up on September 11, 2001, they had plans for the day and perhaps for the future. They had no idea what was in store for them on that day.

This was not so for the 19 hijackers. When Mohammad Atta left his home on that fateful September morning, he knew he would die and take thousands of innocent people with him. He had been planning the September 11 attacks for years. It was a joint effort by several al-Qaeda cells. Al-Qaeda is a terrorist organization led by an Arab militant Islamist, Osama bin Laden. Atta's journey to the World Trade Center did not begin when he boarded AA flight 11 on September 11, 2001. His and the other hijackers' journeys had begun many years before. ⌐

New York City firefighters were among the first responders to the attacks on the World Trade Center.

A firefighter searches through the rubble of the World Trade Center.

A Day in History

rass is now growing at the site of impact just
outside Shanksville, Pennsylvania. The
Pentagon in Arlington, Virginia, has been rebuilt. The
World Trade Center site in New York City has been
cleared of all debris. But the impact of the terrorist

attack on Tuesday, September 11, 2001, can still be felt the world over in international politics and in our daily lives.

There was a time when airline travelers would say good-bye to their loved ones at the terminal. Today, only those with boarding passes are allowed to move beyond the long lines at security checkpoints. Bomb-sniffing dogs are a normal sight at luggage check-in, as are barefoot travelers near airport screening machines. Even a child's sneakers are suspicious.

When those four planes sped toward their demise, they cut through more than concrete and steel; they shook more than the ground. There are days in history that have changed the world. On December 7, 1941, Japanese planes attacked the United States in Pearl Harbor, Hawaii. On June 6, 1944, Allied Forces landed in Normandy, France. On November 22, 1963, John F. Kennedy was shot in Dallas, Texas. These days are etched in the public's consciousness. People who have lived through these days remember precisely where they were and what they were doing. September 11, 2001, is one such day.

"History, despite its wrenching pain, cannot be unlived, but if faced with courage, need not be lived again."[1]

—Maya Angelou

Shaping History

None of these days are isolated. Each has a history that led up to the day as if it were inevitable. These days also have a future, which is to say that the days themselves changed the course of history. After the attack on Pearl Harbor, the United States joined the Allied Forces in World War II. Allied Forces later defeated the Nazis in Normandy on D-Day. John F. Kennedy's assassination changed the course of the Vietnam

---

The Cold War

The term "Cold War" refers to the conflict between the leading communist countries (the Soviet Union and its Eastern allies) and the leading capitalist countries (the United States and its Western allies). It lasted from World War II to the collapse of the Soviet Empire in the 1990s. The term describes the fact that the conflict never became an actual military battle between the two superpowers. Instead, the conflict was characterized by a standoff, with each side threatening the other with nuclear retaliation should it step over the line and attack.

However, there were several smaller conflicts all over the world in which the Soviet Union and the United States fought over dominance of the preferred system of government. The Cold War divided the world into East and West. This is best shown through the actual division of Germany into East Germany and West Germany. Berlin, located in the heart of East Germany, was also divided into East and West. The Berlin Wall, topped with barbed wire and heavily armed guards, sealed off West Berlin from the rest of the country. Hundreds died trying to get from East Berlin to West Berlin. When the wall fell on November 9, 1989, it marked the end of the Cold War.

conflict, which escalated during Lyndon Johnson's presidency.

Indeed, September 11 has a before and an after. Today, September 11 is as relevant as it was that day. Since 9/11, the New York skyline has changed forever and the fear of flying has a whole new dimension. The United States has established the powerful Office of Homeland Security and sent troops to Afghanistan in an all-out War on Terrorism. This move threatened U.S. foreign relations with some of its Western allies. These nations felt there was more than one possible reaction to an event of this magnitude.

Ground Zero

Traditionally the term "Ground Zero" refers to nuclear explosions. It describes the place on the ground directly under the exploding bomb, where the most severe damage occurs. It was originally coined in relation to the nuclear bombings in Nagasaki and Hiroshima during World War II. After the attack on 9/11, the term was adopted quickly for the site of the former World Trade Center.

Afghanistan, one of the countries the U.S. attacked during the War on Terrorism, is arguably where it all began. The history behind 9/11 reaches as far back as the Cold War and its repercussions in the Afghanistan crisis from 1979 to 1989. It includes the Iran-Iraq conflict in the 1980s and its repercussions in the Kuwait invasion in 1990. It draws on the U.S. alliance with Israel and against the Palestinian Liberation

Organization (PLO).

The history behind 9/11 reveals economic issues such as the Western dependence on Middle Eastern oil and the shifting allegiances in international arms trade. It exposes the cultural effects of international trade, and the religious issues of Islam, Christianity, and Judaism in the Middle East.

When Mohammad Atta stepped about AA flight 11 on September 11, 2001, he played a role in a long and complex story full of political, economic, religious, and cultural twists.

The crash site at the Pentagon

Soviet troops in Afghanistan, 1987

The Afghanistan Crisis

On December 24, 1979, the Soviet Union invaded Afghanistan. The goal was to keep the country's communist government in place. The communist People's Democratic Party had overthrown the century-long rule of a royal dynasty in

Afghanistan the year before. The party had adopted atheism rather than Islam and was not welcome by the Muslim population. The Soviet Union had expected a quick invasion. Instead, it faced a long guerilla war from Afghan guerilla fighters, who resented the foreign intrusion.

Afghanistan is a rugged, mountainous country wedged between Iran, Pakistan, and the former Soviet Union. The country is populated by tribal communities with varying cultural and historical connections. They are united by a common religion: Islam.

Afghanistan is a poor country without many natural resources. It was important to the Soviet Union because it is near the oil-rich countries of the Persian Gulf, particularly Iran. More importantly, the Soviet Union was interested in spreading communism worldwide.

Osama bin Laden

Osama bin Laden was born on March 10, 1957, in Riyadh, Saudi Arabia. He was the son of a successful building contractor with close ties to the Saudi royal family. Bin Laden's parents divorced. He grew up with his mother's second husband and was raised as a devout Muslim of the Sunni sect.

This is also why Afghanistan was important to the United States. In 1979, the Cold War divided the world into East and West, communism and capitalism, dictatorship and democracy. The Soviet invasion of

Afghanistan ended the recent détente, an easing of the strained relationship between the United States and the Soviet Union. The United States could not allow the Soviet Union to take over a strategically important place so close to Iran.

Funding the War

The United States viewed the Soviet invasion of Afghanistan as a threat, and spoke out against the foreign occupation of the country. Officially, the United States stayed out of the conflict. Unofficially, the United States supported the anti-Soviet forces by channeling money through Pakistan to the Afghan fighters. Afghanistan was an opportunity for the United States to curb Soviet influence in the Middle East.

Structure of al-Qaeda

The cell structure of al-Qaeda (the Base) is meant to evade detection. Most members of the covert and independent cells will only know the other members in their own cell. Only the leader of a cell will know the leaders of other cells and how to communicate with them. By dividing al-Qaeda into many smaller groups, each of which only knows what it needs to for its individual tasks, the damage of outside discovery can be greatly reduced. Even if one cell has been detected and destroyed, other cells can continue to operate independently. It is this covert cell structure that made it possible for al-Qaeda to operate for so long and on several international stages. They assumed responsibility for many terrorist attacks the world over, not without being detected, but without being destroyed.

U.S. money bought weapons and training for the guerilla warriors. The uprising against the communist government in Afghanistan had originally been fueled by tribal associations among the guerilla groups. The local guerilla war became popular the world over as a *jihad*, a holy war against foreign invaders. Muslim *mujahideen* (religiously motivated fighters) joined the fight from all over the Middle East. By the mid-1980s, Arabic *mullahs* (Muslim clergymen), actively recruited Muslims in other Islamic countries for the holy war in Afghanistan. These mullahs were supported and financed by wealthy Muslim individuals and regions as diverse as Saudi Arabia, Pakistan, Western Europe, and the United States. One of the wealthy Muslims financing and organizing mujahideen was the Saudi Arabian citizen Osama bin Laden. By 1984 Osama bin Laden had founded Maktab al-Khadamat (Office of Order). This organization funneled money, arms, and Muslim fighters from around the world into the Afghan war. Muslim groups from around the world were united

Other al-Qaeda Attacks

Al-Qaeda has claimed responsibility for several terrorist attacks before 9/11. The August 7, 1998, bombings of the United States embassies in Tanzania and Kenya, and the October 2000 attacks in Yemen on the USS *Cole* were al-Qaeda. The February 26, 1993, World Trade Center bombing was carried out by a militant Islamist, but the involvement of al-Qaeda is disputed.

in the fight against the Soviet Union's occupation of Afghanistan.

By 1989, the Soviet Empire was bankrupt. The war had taken its toll on the troops, and they were forced to retreat from Afghanistan. The mujahideen had prevailed and fought back the invaders. The United States considered this a successful Cold War battle won by the West. The mujahideen considered this a successful religious battle won by Muslim (followers of Islam) holy warriors against a secular (not religious) superpower.

A Country Left in Shambles

When the Soviet Union retreated, so did all foreign support. The Afghan guerillas were left alone in a post-war country in shambles. Soon the guerilla groups that had united against a common enemy were divided amongst each other. They returned to old tribal affiliations, warring among themselves. The Afghan civil war raged for years. Then in 1996, one guerilla group, the Taliban, emerged successful and took over the government. The Taliban was organized by mullah Mohammad Omar around a group of fundamentalist Muslim students. Islamic fundamentalism requires a strict adherence to the laws of Islam and a literal interpretation of the Koran. The Taliban turned Afghanistan into a fundamentalist Islamic state, which would not be toppled until 2001.

Unwittingly, U.S. money had financed the seeds for a holy war against another secular superpower: the United States. The fight in Afghanistan had established a common bond among young Muslim men from different Arab countries. It was this common bond that Osama bin Laden was able to exploit in the years to come. By 1988, bin Laden had separated from Maktab al-Khadamat over military differences.

Claiming Responsibility

Al-Qaeda and Osama bin Laden did not officially claim responsibility for the 9/11 attacks until October 2004, one month after the publication of *The 9/11 Commission Report* in September 2004. The report concludes that al-Qaeda was responsible for the attacks.

He left Afghanistan, and went back to his homeland, Saudi Arabia. In the years to come, bin Laden steadily built on the relationships he had established during his years in Afghanistan. He continued funneling money, weapons, and Muslim fighters all over the Middle East, Europe, and the United States. At first, he did so from Saudi Arabia, then from Sudan, and finally from Afghanistan, where he had returned to in 1996. By then, the Taliban was in power, and Afghanistan was an

The Hamburg Cell

The Hamburg cell is the group of radical Islamists who became the key players in the 9/11 attacks. Members included: Mohammad Atta, pilot of AA flight 11; Marwan al-Shehhi, pilot of UA flight 175; and Ramzi Bionashib, who may have been the twentieth hijacker but did not get a visa for the United States.

Islamic state. By this time, Osama bin Laden was a known militant Islamist and terrorist financier. Despite international pressure, the Taliban offered him safety. Eventually, bin Laden's al-Qaeda would emerge as a worldwide network of secret and independent terrorist cells. Each cell contained mujahideen and jihadists willing and ready to give their lives for the cause.

Among them were Mohammad Atta and Khalid Sheikh Mohammad, the suspected mastermind of the 9/11 attacks. These men moved to Germany during the 1990s. They eventually rented an apartment in Hamburg, forming the so-called Hamburg cell of al-Qaeda. They met there on a regular basis, sometimes three to four times a week. They were waiting for their cue to move forward with their plan. ⌐

Mohammad Atta in an al-Qaeda training video

The West Bank Jewish settlement of Shilo, in Israel

U.S. Involvement in the Middle East

On February 23, 1998, Osama bin Laden issued a *fatwa* against the United States. A fatwa is a religious edict, issued by Muslim clerical leaders. However, bin Laden is not a Muslim cleric, or mullah. In conjunction with other Islamic militants, bin Laden's fatwa directed Muslim followers that it was their duty before Allah (Islam's god) to kill civilians and military personnel from the United States and its allies. This would continue until the United States withdrew support for Israel and removed all of its military forces from Islamic countries. They felt that the United States should not be involved in Islamic affairs. The Muslim mujahideen had found a new goal: jihad, a holy war, against the United States.

Bin Laden's fatwa had been long in the making. It came after a long period of U.S. involvement in the Middle East. Bin Laden and his supporters were particularly opposed to U.S. support for Israel and the deployment of U.S. troops in Muslim countries such as Saudi Arabia. He believed these regimes would not be in power without the backing of the U.S. government.

"...we issue the following fatwa to all Muslims: The ruling to kill the Americans and their allies—civilians and military—is an individual duty for every Muslim who can do it in any country in which it is possible to do it, in order to liberate the al-Aqsa Mosque and the holy mosque [Mecca] from their grip, and in order for their armies to move out of all the lands of Islam, defeated and unable to threaten any Muslim. This is in accordance with the words of Almighty God, 'and fight the pagans all together as they fight you all together,' and 'fight them until there is no more tumult or oppression, and there prevail justice and faith in God.'"[1]

—al-Qaeda's fatwa

After the Cold War

During the Cold War, the Middle East had been a large playing field in the race between the United States and the Soviet Union for political and economic influence. Power relations in Europe after World War II were rather clear. Europe was divided into East and West. The Soviet Union ruled the East, and the United States and its allies ruled the West. The Middle East was a different matter. Power relations in that region were up for grabs.

Many of the Arab countries had only just emerged. Both the East and the West had great interest in the Middle East. The Soviet Union shared borders with Middle Eastern states such as Iran and Afghanistan. The region's oil

Interview with bin Laden

On December 23, 1998, *Time* magazine interviewed Osama bin Laden. The reporter questioned bin Laden about the bombings of the U.S. embassies in Tanzania and Kenya. When asked whether he was responsible, bin Laden responded:

The International Islamic Front for Jihad against the U.S. and Israel has issued a crystal-clear fatwa calling on the Islamic nation to carry on jihad aimed at liberating holy sites. The nation of Muhammad has responded to this appeal. If the instigation for jihad against the Jews and the Americans in order to liberate Al-Aqsa Mosque and the Holy Ka'aba [Islamic shrines in the Middle East] is considered a crime, then let history be a witness that I am a criminal. Our job is to instigate and, by the grace of God, we did that—and certain people responded to this instigation.[2]

resources were important to both the Soviet Union and to the United States and its allies. Also, the local military disagreements among the new Middle Eastern nations would be a major market for the arms trade.

By the time bin Laden issued the fatwa, the Soviet empire had collapsed. But the relationships that the United States and the Soviet Union had pursued in the Middle East during the Cold War had created attitudes that lasted well beyond its end.

Muslim states were more inclined to side with the Soviet Union. They were drawn to the socialist organization of the economy and dictatorial leadership style. However, many Middle Eastern countries were wary of both the Soviet Union and the United States.

The one country close to the United States in its economic, political, and social structure was, and still is, Israel. Like the United States, Israel is a free market economy, based on democracy. Israel also had potential strategic importance should the Cold War ever end in the Middle East. The United States and Israel became faithful allies.

> "What is objectionable, what is dangerous, about extremists is not that they are extreme, but that they are intolerant. The evil is not what they say about their cause, but what they say about their opponents."[3]
>
> —*Robert F. Kennedy*

ISRAEL

Israel is the only Jewish state in the Middle East. It is constantly engaged in territorial disputes with the Muslim Arab world. The dispute has complex historical, political, and religious roots. The three major religions, Judaism, Christianity, and Islam, each lay claim on the region of Palestine. Palestine is the area between the Mediterranean Sea and the river Jordan. All three religions consider Jerusalem, the capital of Israel, a holy city. The area has been fought over since Biblical times. It has been ruled by each religion at varying points in history.

At the end of the nineteenth century, the Zionist movement was established. It aimed to create a national homeland for Jews in Palestine. A large number of Eastern European and German Jewish immigrants moved to Palestine during the 1930s and 1940s. Zionist leaders claimed a historical connection to the area, since their ancestors had lived in Palestine 2,000 years earlier. The Arab people of Palestine felt that a Jewish state would be a violation of their historical rights in the region. It would also make an independent Palestinian state impossible. In 1948, Israel declared its independence. Prior struggles between the Zionists and the Muslim Palestinians and their supporters immediately escalated into a full-scale Arab-Israeli war.

At first, the United States did not support Israel in the Arab-Israeli war of 1948. This was during the Cold War. At that time, it was clear that support of Israel would tilt the attitudes of the Muslim Arab world against the United States and toward the Soviet Union. However, when the Soviet Union supported the Arab attack against Israel, the United States put its resources behind Israel. From this point onward, through all conflicts, the United States has supported Israel—diplomatically, politically, financially, and at times even with its military.

FBI's Ten Most Wanted

In 1998, Osama bin Laden made the FBI's Ten Most Wanted List. He is considered responsible for the August 7, 1998, bombings of the U.S. embassies in Tanzania and Kenya. He is not officially wanted for the 9/11 attacks.

The Soviet Union, on the other hand, has supported the Palestinian Liberation Organization (PLO), the major opponent of Israel. The PLO was founded in 1964 by the Arab League of Nations. It aimed to liberate Palestine from Israeli occupation. In 1974, the United Nations (UN) accepted the PLO as the legitimate representative of the Palestinian people. It has been an observer in the UN Assembly ever since. The UN reaffirmed the rights of the people of Palestine to self-determination, independence, and to return to Palestine. In 1988, the PLO officially adopted a two-state solution, with Israel and Palestine living side by side. However, many Palestinian leaders still consider the liberation of all of Palestine their ultimate goal.

THE PERSIAN GULF WAR

The bond between the United States and Israel, and the anti-American attitudes among militant Muslim Arabs, became apparent in 1990. During the Persian Gulf War, Iraqi President Saddam Hussein threatened to attack Israel if the United States came to Kuwait's aid. Hussein hoped that by including Israel in the conflict, the Muslim Arab world would support him.

Kuwait is a small country on the coast of the Persian Gulf. It is bordered by Saudi Arabia to the south and Iraq to the north. Its natural oil resources make the country important far beyond its size. On August 2, 1990, Hussein's military forces overtook Kuwait and assumed control of the government.

Slant Drilling

Originally, drilling for oil could only be done by drilling straight down into the ground. The slant drilling method allows drilling at an angle. As a result, a drill may enter the ground in one country, only to slant underground, cross a border, and remove oil from another country.

U.S. Secretary of Defense Richard Cheney meets with Kuwait Defense Minister Ali Sabah, May 7, 1991.

Hussein claimed that Kuwaiti territory was an Iraqi province and that Kuwait had been slant drilling into Iraqi oil supplies. The UN and many of its Arab member nations criticized Hussein's aggression. The Arab nations were worried about Hussein seeking dominance in the region. The West, led by the United States, feared for its oil. Yet economic sanctions and diplomacy led nowhere. The UN Security Council authorized a coalition of 34 nations to fight what is now known as the Persian Gulf War. After six weeks, the coalition forced Iraq to withdraw its troops from Kuwait on February 26, 1991.

The United States had supported Saddam Hussein in the Iran-Iraq war between 1980 and 1988. The United States had been wary of Iran since the Islamic revolution in 1979. Shah Mohammed Pahlevi had been ousted and replaced by a fundamentalist Islamist regime under Ayatollah Khomeini. At virtually the same time, the Soviets were invading Afghanistan, a neighbor to Iran. Clearly, the motives for U.S. involvement in the Middle East lay extremely close together: to curb Soviet influence in the Middle East, and to curb the spread of Islamic fundamentalism. By supporting Hussein in the 1980s, the United States had unwittingly helped the dictator who later attacked Kuwait.

U.S. PRESENCE

Following the Gulf War, the United States received continued support from Arab countries such as Saudi Arabia. Yet the war had brought attention to U.S. involvement in the Middle East.

When Iraq invaded Kuwait in 1990, bin Laden had offered his own men to help defend Saudi Arabian borders against Iraqi aggression. The Saudi Arabian government rejected his offer. Instead, Saudi Arabia allowed the U.S.-led UN coalition to establish military bases on Saudi ground. Angered, bin Laden spoke out against his government's dependence on U.S. military. He demanded an end to foreign military bases in the country.

The presence of U.S. forces in Saudi Arabia after the Gulf War angered the Muslim community. Saudi Arabia is home to the sacred Muslim cities of Mecca and Medina. The Saudi monarchy came under attack from Islamist extremists. Bin Laden and his supporters felt that Saudi Arabia and other U.S.-backed regimes would crumble if not for the continued U.S. support. Therefore, they felt action must first be taken against the United States directly.

Osama bin Laden and al-Qaeda

Bin Laden's criticism of the Saudi government made him unwelcome in his homeland. In 1991, bin Laden was forced to leave Saudi Arabia. He moved his organization to Sudan. By the mid-1990s, bin Laden's militant Islamist views were well known. He was a suspected terrorist. In 1996, he was forced to leave Sudan as well. He returned to Afghanistan. There, he was welcomed by the Taliban government, which had taken over the country. By 1997, bin Laden had established a wide network of al-Qaeda training camps, headquartered in Afghanistan. On February 23, 1998, bin Laden and other militant Islamic leaders issued the fatwa.

In 1999 Mohammad Atta reportedly visited an al-Qaeda training camp in Afghanistan. *The 9/11 Commission Report* states that the original plan had called for longtime members of al-Qaeda to carry out the attack on 9/11. Because the members of the Hamburg cell spoke English well and had adapted to the Western lifestyle, the plan was changed. The Hamburg cell moved to the United States, where it would be easier to prepare the attacks. On September 11, 2001, Atta and 18 other hijackers carried out one battle in the holy war that Osama bin Laden had declared in the fatwa.

Al-Qaeda leader Osama bin Laden in April 1998

An American flag and an Israeli flag are burned during a demonstration.

ANTI-AMERICAN
SENTIMENTS

ince 9/11 there have been tendencies, both political and personal, to vilify Osama bin Laden by calling him a criminal and his fatwa the ramblings of a madman. But to ignore his complaints about perceived U.S. offenses against the Islamic people is to ignore the feelings of the Muslim world. The United States supported Israel for decades and in essence denied the rights of the Muslim Arabs to Palestine. The United States sent troops to Saudi Arabia during the Persian Gulf War and threatened military intervention in Iraq. The United States tried to control the affairs of several nations in a region that perhaps should have been beyond its control.

Complaints Against U.S. Involvement

Since 9/11, there also have been political and personal tendencies to criticize the United States. The U.S. intervention in the Middle East has been labeled as a self-serving attempt to establish economic and political dominance. But to ignore the self-appointed role of the United States as a guardian of democracy is to ignore a legitimate desire to help establish peace and universal acceptance of human rights. Adopting a policy of non-involvement would also have meant

Oil-based Economy

The economies of countries belonging to OPEC (Organization of the Petroleum Exporting Countries) rely almost entirely on oil. Kuwait holds ten percent of the world's petroleum reserves. Petroleum accounts for almost 50 percent of Kuwait's Gross Domestic Product (GDP) and for 95 percent of its export revenues. Saudi Arabia holds 25 percent of the world's petroleum reserves. Petroleum accounts for 45 percent of Saudi Arabia's GDP, and 90 percent of its export earnings.

turning away from the peace process between Israel and the PLO.

By becoming involved in the Middle East, the United States clearly offended some Arabs. However, a nation as powerful as the United States cannot simply remove itself from international affairs. The United States is a major player in the global economy. It also has a responsibility that goes beyond finding new markets or importing and exporting goods. It is the responsibility to recognize that trade relations have powerful political, social, and cultural implications.

At the beginning of the Cold War, the Middle East was a region with untapped political alliances. The United States and the Soviet Union

Coca-Cola in the Middle East

Coca-Cola has taken on symbolic importance as an image representing the United States. The Coca-Cola Company was the target of anti-Americanism in the Middle East.

In 2000, critics of Coca-Cola in Egypt claimed that the label contained the anti-Islamist slogans "No Muhammad," and "No Mekka." They called upon devout Muslims to boycott the soft drink. Coca-Cola claims that sales dropped by ten percent.

The rumor was not squashed until the Grand Mufti of Egypt (one of the highest religious leaders in the country), admitted that he enjoyed at least a can of Coke a day.

In 2003 a French entrepreneur launched Mekka Cola. The product is advertised as a "buy Muslim" alternative to Coca-Cola for devout Muslims.

both wanted to sway the region in their favor. The Middle East was also an untapped market. The United States and the Soviet Union were especially interested in buying oil and selling arms in the Middle East.

TRADE RELATIONS IN THE MIDDLE EAST

After World War II, the Middle East was politically unstable. Many of the nations had only just become independent. Many nations were centuries-old monarchies. Other nations were quickly emerging from tribal dynasties. Saudi Arabia and Jordan are monarchies to this day. Monarchies in Egypt and Iraq were overthrown during the 1950s. Over the decades that followed, many of these regimes became more and more dictatorial. They often violently repressed any opposition. As a reaction, Muslims united under their faith, in opposition to these regimes.

Iraq's Economy

In the 1990s, Iraq's economy and agriculture were under severe strain. Economic sanctions from the UN forced Iraq to decrease the size of its army. To ease the situation of the population, the UN developed the oil-for-food program in 1995. It allowed Iraq to sell oil despite the economic sanctions in exchange for food and medicine. However, this program was corrupt from the beginning. Funds were skimmed and fraud was common. The program was abolished in 2003, when the United States invaded Iraq as part of the War on Terrorism.

The United States engaged in trade relations with many countries in the Middle East, often with disregard for the way the government might treat its citizens. The United States had trade relations with dictators such as Saddam Hussein in Iraq and monarchs like Shah Mohammed Reza Pahlavi in Iran. The idea was to pave the way for political influence. However, the countries in question did not necessarily adopt democracy in return for American weapons. The United States supported the Shah of Iran for three decades, from the 1950s through the 1970s, for fear that the Iranian Communist Party would take over. In 1979, Pahlavi was overthrown by an even more repressive regime under Ayatollah Khomeini. In the 1980s, the United States supported Hussein's Iraq against Khomeini's Iran. It wanted to curb the Islamic extremism that had toppled Shah Pahlavi. However, Hussein would later attack Kuwait in 1990, threatening the fragile stability of the entire Middle East. To the Arab people, U.S. trade with nations such as Iran and Iraq was proof of a double standard. The United States spoke of freedom,

Many cities in Iraq were devastated during the Gulf War.

democracy, and human rights while shaking hands and making deals with dictators such as Hussein.

MIDDLE EASTERN WEALTH AND POVERTY

The U.S. arms trade may have helped support a system of shifting political alliances. However, the oil trade might also have helped create a region with a struggling economy. At first, the incredible wealth that countries such as Saudi Arabia and Kuwait gained by exporting oil created an economic boom. State-sponsored modernization projects, social welfare systems, and educational programs emerged. These projects were meant to help countries overcome third-world status as quickly as possible.

Over the years, these programs could not be kept going. The reliance on oil did not allow the emerging economies to grow. Many state-sponsored projects were dropped, leading to massive unemployment. This, in turn, led to a growing economic gap between a rich ruling class and a population struggling with poverty. Despite the oil boom, the living standard of the Muslim population in the Middle East left much to be desired.

This only helped feed resentment, frustration, and outrage against the United States. The Middle East remained a third-world region while the United States was becoming the most powerful country in the world.

The Ottoman Empire

Arab resentment of these power relations runs deeper than plain economic jealousy. It goes back to the fact that today's power relations are a reversal of fortune of historic proportions. The Ottoman Empire was once the center for arts and sciences, and Muslims controlled trade routes between continents. The empire stretched from Spain and northern Africa to China and India. It was established in 1299 and continued to gain power through the sixteenth century. The empire was pursuing modernization while strictly following the principles of Islam. Islam united the diverse cultural groups that made up the Ottoman Empire, as much as Christianity united central and northern Europe.

At the time when they controlled much of the trade between Europe and Asia and were advancing in scholarly activities, Muslims saw their success as proof that Islam was the true faith.

Over the centuries the Ottoman Empire fell apart, and the Christian European nation-states grew in importance. In 1922, after World War I, the empire officially collapsed. The British and French ruled the Middle East. Then came the battle over the region in the Cold War era. When the Cold War was over, the United States took control over global trade. The United States also became home to the latest advances in science and art.

An upscale American department store, Saks Fifth Avenue, inside the Kingdom shopping mall in Riyadh, Saudi Arabia, July, 2002.

CHRISTIAN AND MUSLIM VALUES

The huge amount of American consumer goods, art, movies, and music available all over the world, including the Middle East, speaks of U.S. economic dominance. The presence of Coca-Cola, Andy Warhol,

McDonald's, Hollywood, Timex watches, Ford, GMC, the American language, and the American dollar are all signs of how the United States has influenced economies around the world. Many Americans believe that the global success of the United States justifies its dominance.

Along with its products, the United States exports its values. This is not always intended, but it is an unavoidable and, perhaps, even desired by-product known as "Americanization." Part of the original idea behind trade relations was to pave the way for political, social, and cultural change.

Yet to many Muslims in the Middle East, the values America exports are not valuable. American government is intended to be secular, whereas Muslims draw deeply from their religion in all aspects of their lives, including politics and government. Life, liberty, and the pursuit of happiness are the inalienable rights etched in the U.S. Declaration of Independence. These rights direct individuals toward self-fulfillment. To Muslims, life is primarily a spiritual experience, navigated by religious duties. In the Muslim world, self-fulfillment does not feature wealth, success, and physical beauty. Freedom, democracy, and self-expression have no room in the traditional patriarchal society. Muslim society is based not on a secular political philosophy but on Islamic law laid down in the Koran.

Many Muslims feel that Americanization distracts them from the ultimate goal and true basis of their existence: faith. For Muslims, the historical reversal of fortune is a sign that it is time to change their ways and return more deeply to Islamic values. Many Muslims believe the American way is the wrong way, the immoral way away from Allah.

These attitudes were fertile ground for Osama bin Laden. Poverty and years of political oppression had created an explosive atmosphere of discontent among the Muslim population. He was riding high on a wave of anti-American sentiment and the power of Islamic fundamentalism. He used the Muslim world's complaints about U.S. military, political, and cultural influence, and exploited them to his ends. Religious zeal became his primary recruiting tool. Many young Muslim men chose the jihad and its promise of a better life in death over life with little hope for an economically successful future. Mohammad Atta was among their recruits.

Pakistan's religious schools teach students about jihad.

Islamic worshippers pray during a service on the first day of Ramadan.

THE ORIGINS OF JIHAD

Osama bin Laden is not a cleric. Still, his interpretation of Allah's words resonated greatly in the Muslim world. His words expressed a long-held bitterness over economic misery and perceived threats to the Islamic way of life. He had also proven himself a successful leader in the holy war in Afghanistan. His al-Qaeda network was steadily growing into a well-financed, well-trained, and well-connected organization. To many young, devout Muslims, he was the man of the future. But it is important to remember that even though he has many followers, bin Laden's interpretation of Islam is not a version accepted or believed by the majority of Muslims.

Islamic clergy

Muhammad did not set up a formal church. Therefore, there are no priests between the individual believer and Allah in Islam. Every Muslim has direct access to and immediate responsibility before Allah. Islamic clergy are the guardians of tradition and ritual. They are not the representatives of Allah on Earth.

ISLAM

Islam is the youngest of the three religions founded in the Middle East. Christianity and Judaism are the other two. Over 1 billion people all over the world call themselves Muslims. Muslims are followers of the Islamic faith. Islam originated with the teaching of the prophet Muhammad. He united the many tribes of Arabia under Islamic law. Muhammad died in 632, yet his religion is powerful to this day.

Islam is not fundamentally different from Judaism and Christianity. All three religions are monotheistic, which means they believe in only one God. Allah is the

Muslim name of God. They also all accept the same prophets, all the way back to Abraham. Islam simply holds that Muhammad was the last prophet and received the word of Allah directly from Allah. The Koran is the word of Allah. Therefore, it is decisive and definitive. It covers all aspects of life—private and public, legal and administrative, and of course, religious. Faith is the pillar of every devout Muslim's life, because they will be rewarded for their faith on Judgment Day.

The West may criticize Islam for the unequal position of women in Islamic societies and the seemingly closed-minded idea that the Koran must not be interpreted, but

Head Wear

Many Muslim women wear a veil covering their faces. Many Westerners view this as a sign that women are oppressed in Islamic cultures. Women remain hidden behind the veil, and thus "invisible" to society. They have little or no influence on public life. Most Middle Eastern states have not adopted the Western notion of gender equality. The Koran allows for unequal treatment of women.

Yet the Koran also allows for change. Women in Turkey, a country with strong Islamic traditions, are afforded much the same rights as men. In other words, whether women are oppressed has more to do with a country's social structure than with religious convictions.

Religion is often used as a reason to keep alive traditional social structures that help keep a government in power. Head wear has a long-standing tradition in many religions. Sikh men wear a turban, Jewish men wear a kippah, and the Roman Catholic clergy wear a zuchetto. Most headwear is a sign of respect for God, purity, and chastity.

taken as law. However, Islam cannot be criticized as a ready blueprint for Osama bin Laden's aggressive terrorist warfare. His hateful tirades against the United States and Israel, his disdain for Christians and Jews, and his obvious disregard for human life are his own. Another principle of Islam is that the Muslim community is made up of all those who serve Allah. Regardless of their racial or national origin, their language or social status, every man is equal before Allah.

Jihad

It is widely held that the jihadists willingly proceeded to their death because they believed that their heroism would be rewarded in an afterlife. During training, Jihad recruiters described what rewards would await the potential martyr in paradise.

THE FIVE PILLARS OF ISLAM

Muslim life is structured around the five pillars of Islam. These are the five official duties before Allah:

❖ to accept the fact that Allah is great and that Muhammad was the last prophet

❖ to abide by the prayer ritual five times a day

❖ to share personal wealth by giving to charity

❖ to fast during Ramadan

❖ to undertake pilgrimage to Mecca at least once in an individual's lifetime

A small group of Afghan mujahideen kneel on prayer rugs in the desert sand in Khafji, Saudi Arabia.

Some, Osama bin Laden among them, claim that there is a sixth. That sixth duty is jihad. Jihad stems from an Arabic verb meaning to struggle, or to persevere. The term refers to the struggle of the individual to live in the way of Allah, to live a devout Muslim life, abiding by all principles and pillars of Islam. Jihad primarily refers to the struggle of the soul against adverse forces within.

Yet life in the way of Allah includes a promise to uphold the faith. Thus, jihad is the struggle against outside forces in the defense of Islam. Jihad as warfare is allowed in order to fight injustice and oppression by the enemies of Islam, but only after it has been made clear that they have committed these injustices. In other words, jihad as a holy war is to be the last resort. This is the portion of Islam that Osama bin Laden focused on in his call to arms for a holy war against the mortal enemies of Islam: the United States and Israel.

FAITH TO JUSTIFY VIOLENCE

Using faith as justification for warfare is not new, nor is it unique to Islam. Christians were waging war for 200 years during the Crusades between 1095 and 1291. They were sent by their popes to defend and spread Christianity.

However, Osama bin Laden is not the primary religious leader of Islam. In fact, he is not even a cleric and has no official legitimacy as a guardian of Islam.

A terrorist act is any violent act that targets civilians, is meant to spread terror in the name of a cause, and has not been committed by a legitimate government. That, among other things, brands him a terrorist rather than a warrior.

The UN has defined terrorism as any act,

"Islam, as practiced by the vast majority of people, is a peaceful religion, a religion that respects others. Ours is a country based upon tolerance and we welcome people of all faiths in America."[2]

— *George W. Bush*

intended to cause death or serious bodily harm to civilians or non-combatants with the purpose of intimidating a population or compelling a government or an international organization to do or abstain from doing any act.[1]

Terrorism is motivated by a desire to force political change or call attention to a cause. Terror and fear are meant as a wake-up call to those standing in the way of the terrorist's goals. Terrorists believe in the righteousness of their cause. They believe that their ends justify their means. Violent acts killing innocent bystanders, while regrettable, are considered a necessary evil. Terrorists see themselves as freedom fighters, revolutionaries, guerillas, or rebels. They see themselves as holy warriors, mujahideen, or jihadists.

MOTIVATION OF JIHAD

Osama bin Laden's jihadists believe that they are on the side of good (Islam) against evil (Judaism and Christianity). They believe that their plight, Muslim's lack of control of the Middle East, has been ignored.

This is shown clearly through continued U.S. support for Israel. They believe that striking at the symbols of their enemy's power will call attention to their cause. As their culture and way of life seems threatened, they turn to jihad as a last resort.

> "The terrorists are traitors to their own faith, trying, in effect, to hijack Islam itself. The enemy of America is not our many Muslim friends; it is not our many Arab friends. Our enemy is a radical network of terrorists, and every government that supports them."[3]
>
> — *George W. Bush*

As a defense against an enemy that threatens their faith, they feel jihad is acceptable. In fact, it is an act of heroism and honor. A jihadist is a martyr who will be rewarded in the afterlife.

Mohammad Atta, Hani Hanjour, Marwan al Shehhi, Ziad Jarrah, and the other jihadists who stepped on those planes on 9/11 were not psychopathic criminals, suicidal maniacs, or social deviants. They were ordinary people from rather unremarkable backgrounds. They came from different countries and from families with varying social statuses. Some of them were well educated and had lived and studied in the West among family and friends for years. They were motivated by their frustrations with the political and economic situation in the Middle East and by their hatred for the United States and Israel and their firm belief that their actions would help the Islamic world rise to greatness yet again.

Understanding September 11

Knowing the history makes the events of 9/11 so much more complex. It seems impossible to pick out a terrorist. It seems possible that given the right circumstance, a leader such as Osama bin Laden might find the right words to turn anyone into a terrorist. The attacks of 9/11 had a history. Those who carried out the attacks had their reasons.

The question then is: does the sum of those reasons justify the killing and maiming of civilians and innocent bystanders? Under International Law, abiding by the UN Charter of Universal Human Rights, the answer is no. These documents state the belief shared by most people in the world that "everyone has the right to life, liberty and security of person."[4]

The utter disregard for human life that goes with terrorism is not justifiable. In part, that is precisely why terrorism is so powerful. It strikes at the very core of humanity—the belief that every human life is sacred.

The history of and reasons for the attacks must be explored. It is important to understand how individual U.S. policies and attitudes may have played into the terrorists' hands.

*Afghan refugees were told by the Taliban to leave their homes after the
September 11 terrorist attacks in New York and Washington, D.C.*

Survivors of the World Trade Center attacks help each other through the rubble.

WE ARE ALL AMERICANS

On September 11, 2001, at 10:30 a.m., the Twin Towers lay in ruins. Disbelief, shock, and horror were quickly followed by an outpouring of solidarity and support. Firefighters, emergency crews, police, and civilians were assisting each other while running from the debris. There are stories of people carrying those who could not run; stories of people stopping to give first aid before resuming to run. There were people sharing blankets and jackets to stay warm. They shared tissues to wipe off the tears or the soot or the blood.

It did not stop with those who were directly involved. Within hours, people and search-and-rescue teams from all over Manhattan and the rest of New York came to lend a hand. People came to donate blood and give medical assistance.

When there was no more need for any search, no more chance of any rescue, people from all over the United States and from all over the world arrived in New York to help clean up. Workers carted off the jagged mountain of rubble and steel.

Rubble

More than 1.5 million tons of rubble were removed from Ground Zero.

It was slow, careful, painstaking work. They carried off the dead. They found body parts. They picked through the debris, careful not to miss a ring, a shirt, or a cell phone. They tried to salvage anything that might have survived the attack. They saved anything they could give to those left behind. The work was difficult, both physically and emotionally. Workers involved in the cleanup put their own health at risk, breathing the dust and asbestos in the air.

North Atlantic Treaty Organization

The North Atlantic Treaty Organization (NATO) is a military alliance that was formed in 1949. It originally established an alliance against perceived Soviet aggression in eastern Europe and the North Atlantic, but has since admitted a number of countries that were once part of the former Soviet Union. The treaty reads in part:

"*The Parties agree that an armed attack against one or more of them in Europe or North America shall be considered an attack against them all and consequently they agree that, if such an armed attack occurs, each of them, in exercise of the right of individual or collective self-defence recognised by Article 51 of the Charter of the United Nations, will assist the Party or Parties so attacked by taking forthwith, individually and in concert with the other Parties, such action as it deems necessary, including the use of armed force, to restore and maintain the security of the North Atlantic area. Any such armed attack and all measures taken as a result thereof shall immediately be reported to the Security Council. Such measures shall be terminated when the Security Council has taken the measures necessary to restore and maintain international peace and security.*"[1]

"WE ARE ALL AMERICANS"

Outside of New York, Washington D.C., and Shanksville, Pennsylvania, people found other ways to show their support. Within days, relief funds were set up that would eventually collect millions of dollars from all over the world. In places across the globe, people were embracing each other at makeshift shrines and lighting candles in remembrance of the dead. The European Union declared Friday, September 14, 2001, a day of mourning. All Europeans were asked to observe three minutes of silence at noon. The American flag was raised in storefronts and private homes and adorned cars and backpacks all over the world. In Great Britain, by royal order, the American anthem was played during the changing of the guard at Buckingham Palace.

Respiratory Problems

On September 5, 2006, a study conducted by the Mount Sinai Medical Center in New York reported that the workers and volunteers who cleaned up the World Trade Center site suffered health problems resulting from their work at Ground Zero. Working among the debris, the dust, the smoke, and the fumes left an unusually high proportion of relief workers and volunteers with chronic respiratory problems.

The attacks were headline news all over the world. Newspapers and magazines spoke of the disbelief and outrage over the attacks, expressing solidarity and support for the United States. The September 12, 2001, edition of *Le Monde* in Paris summed it up, "We are all Americans." The world rallied together. Leaders from Europe, Russia, China, Japan, Korea, and other nations sent their condolences and expressed their support. So did leaders from the Middle East. Egypt, Palestine, and Libya all condemned the attacks, and spoke out against terrorism and in support of the United States.

President Bush gave an address to the nation on the evening of September 11, 2001. His strong words were echoed and backed up on the highest international levels. UN Secretary-General Kofi Annan resolved to provide the framework for an international campaign against terrorism. Perhaps the most significant display of support came from then NATO Secretary-General Lord Robertson. Robertson asked the alliance's 19 member states to invoke Article 5 of its charter. This action meant that NATO would view the attacks on the United States as an attack on them all. This would give them license to use military force against the terrorists who had attacked the United States. In short, he offered the military support of the most powerful military alliance in the world. Summed up in the slogan of the day, "United we stand," the attack was viewed not as an attack against the United States, but as an attack against all of humanity.

Perceptions of the Middle East

There was a darker side to the story as well. The Bush administration was quick to identify Osama bin Laden as the mastermind behind the attack. Taliban leaders in Afghanistan were suspected of harboring bin Laden at the al-Qaeda headquarters. Al-Qaeda reacted

*People leave flowers and photos at a makeshift memorial
to honor the victims of September 11.*

evasively. They claimed that there was no proof that the
organization was even involved. Meanwhile, images of
Muslims dancing in the streets of Middle Eastern towns
were shown on American television. Muslims burning
the American flag in celebration of the attacks flickered
on international television.

In the United States, the attacks gave rise to a wave of hate crimes (crimes motivated by prejudice) against people of Middle Eastern descent. The incidents included verbal abuse, physical assault, arson, vandalism at places of worship, death threats, and even murder. On September 15, 2001, Balbir Singh Sodhi was killed. His assailants thought he was a Muslim because he wore a turban. Turbans are the traditional headwear of the Sikh. Sodhi was from India.

Hate crimes are not condoned by a majority of the American people. Yet they spread an atmosphere of fear through the Muslim population of the United States in the aftermath of 9/11.

September 11, 2001, changed the world. The effects of that change on personal lives, society, politics, economy, and culture in the United States and abroad are still elusive.

Pakistani women pray during a U.S. bombing of Afghanistan.

An aircraft takes off on a mission in support of Operation Iraqi Freedom.

INTERNATIONAL ISSUES

On October 7, 2001, Operation Enduring Freedom began. It involved an aerial bombing campaign against Afghanistan that targeted the Taliban and al-Qaeda. This military operation was part of the War on Terrorism declared by President

Bush on national television on the evening of September 11, 2001.

OPERATION ENDURING FREEDOM

The goal of Operation Enduring Freedom was to capture Osama bin Laden and to bring down the Taliban government. According to *The 9/11 Commission Report*, the strike against the Taliban government was both a retaliation and a preventive measure. The organization suspected of harboring Osama bin Laden had not met demands to deliver him. The bombing was meant to warn Afghanistan against offering a home to terrorists in the future.

"The search is underway for those who are behind these evil acts. I've directed the full resources of our intelligence and law enforcement communities to find those responsible and to bring them to justice. We will make no distinction between the terrorists who committed these acts and those who harbor them."[1]

—*George W. Bush*

Operation Enduring Freedom was a NATO-authorized strike led by the United States, Great Britain, and the Afghan Northern Alliance. Many other countries have provided support over the years. Operation Enduring Freedom was not successful in capturing Osama bin Laden. Yet the military intervention did succeed in bringing down the Taliban government. Democratic elections in 2005 were signs of hope despite ongoing guerilla wars.

THE BUSH DOCTRINE

Operation Enduring Freedom was the first military action in line with *The National Security Strategy of the United States of America*. This document is also called the Bush Doctrine. It calls for military preemption and independent action and a commitment to bring freedom, democracy, peace, and security to the world.

The policy was in line with President Bush's words on September 11, 2001: "We will make no distinction between the terrorists who committed these acts and those who harbor them."[2]

Treatment of Prisoners

The War on Terrorism has produced several scandals involving the treatment of prisoners by American soldiers. The Guantanamo Bay Detainment Camp in Cuba holds prisoners suspected of involvement in terrorist organizations. The detainment camp has come under severe criticism because prisoners were held without trial and were allegedly interrogated under torture. Both of these actions infringe upon the rights of prisoners of war under the Geneva Convention.

On April 28, 2004, *60 Minutes II* reported torture and abuse of prisoners in the Abu Ghraib prison in Iraq. The abuse included graphic images of American soldiers abusing prisoners. The U.S. Department of Defense removed the individuals involved from duty and put them on trial. Several soldiers were convicted of charges of abuse. The scandal severely damaged the image of the United States. To many, the prisoner abuse was proof of a general attitude of disrespect and disdain for Arabs, contradicting the cultural tolerance proclaimed by America.

The Bush Doctrine formed the basis for the all-out war on terror. The goals of this war include: preventing terrorist groups from launching attacks, putting an end to state funding of terrorism, and spreading democracy to all corners of the world. The means of this war include: diplomacy, economic sanctions, stopping the financial support system of terrorist organizations, international police action against known terrorists, domestic preparedness, and military action abroad.

The War on Terrorism was cast as a war of values. It is a war against political oppression and religious fundamentalism and in defense of democracy and human rights. While many people agreed with the Bush Doctrine at first, its practical use soon became a subject of debate. Two main issues are disputed: preemptive military action (invading a country that has not declared war), and regime change (bringing down a government in an

Death Toll

In September 2006, close to the fifth anniversary of the attacks, the death toll of the War on Terrorism had surpassed that of the attacks themselves. A total of 2,974 U.S. military service members had been killed in the War on Terrorism (329 in Operation Enduring Freedom; 2,645 in Operation Iraqi Freedom), compared to the 2,973 Americans and foreign nationals who perished in the attacks, excluding the terrorists. The number of casualties among the Afghan and Iraqi military and civilian population is estimated in the hundreds of thousands.

independent country in order to
introduce democracy). Both issues
drew attention due to the Iraq war.

Operation Iraqi Freedom

The Iraq war began with the U.S.
invasion on March 20, 2003. The
United States began Operation Iraqi
Freedom after Saddam Hussein
refused to submit to UN inspection
of his weapons program. Iraq was
considered a rogue state with a
potentially large weapons arsenal.
It was also suspected to possess weapons of mass
destruction that had been outlawed in 1992.

Before the invasion, the United States, supported by
Great Britain, sought support of the UN Security
Council for military intervention against Iraq. They
withdrew the request before a vote came to pass.
France, Russia, and China had made it clear that they
would not support the use of military force in Iraq.

The Iraq war threatened the relationship of the
United States and its allies greatly, less than a year after
the September 11 attacks and the outpouring of support
in their wake. Bush defined Iraq as part of the so-called

Failed State

The Fund for Peace, a U.S.
think tank, publishes a
yearly Failed State Index.
Failed states are politically
unstable states in which
the government has little
to no control over much
of its territory. In 2006,
Iraq was fourth on that list.
Afghanistan was tenth.

Axis of Evil (Iraq, Iran, and North Korea), and the intervention part of the war against terrorism. Under the Bush Doctrine, this made it possible for the U.S. military to strike first, without a declaration of war by Hussein.

The declared goal of the intervention was to remove Hussein from power and to force a regime change in Iraq. Critics voiced concern that a forced regime change violates the rights of an independent nation. In part, the rift among U.S. allies widened because of the harsh language used by the U.S. government during this conflict. As President Bush stated,

> *Every nation, in every region, now has a decision to make. Either you are with us, or you are with the terrorists.*[3]

Statements such as this one were used time and again. They meant to say that sides had to be chosen. The United States made the conflict "us" versus "them." Bush and his supporters seemed to expect total support rather than critical partners in a war against a common enemy. On May 1, 2003, President Bush declared the end of major combat in Iraq in his famous "Mission Accomplished" speech. At the time, Hussein had been removed from office but not captured. U.S. troops would face military attacks for years to come.

U.S. Relations in the Middle East

Many temporary governments, each monitored by
the United States, followed Hussein's capture on
December 13, 2003. These temporary governments
only increased Iraqi resistance. Opposition came from
supporters of Hussein's Ba'ath party, militant Islamists
supported by al-Qaeda, and general opposition to the
foreign invasion. In June 2004, a democratically
elected government took office. However, Iraq remains
a politically unstable country. There is a constant threat
of civil war and of guerilla attacks on the foreign forces
still stationed there.

Saddam Hussein was put on trial in Iraqi court on
October 19, 2005, two years after his capture. He was
convicted of war crimes and sentenced to death on
November 5, 2006. He was executed on December 30,
2006.

Saddam Hussein addresses the court during his trial in 2006.

Protesters demonstrate against the war in Iraq.

Domestic Issues

O n October 26, 2001, President George
W. Bush signed the Patriot Act (the
Uniting and Strengthening America by Providing
Appropriate Tools Required to Intercept and Obstruct
Terrorism Act of 2001) into law. The Patriot Act

greatly expanded the authority of law enforcement officials to bring terrorists to justice at home.

THE PATRIOT ACT

At first, the Patriot Act found widespread approval among the U.S. population. However, its intrusion on civil liberties became subject of much criticism. The controversial parts of the Patriot Act restrict due process of law (proper legal procedures entitled to citizens) for individuals involved with, or suspected of being involved with, terrorism. The Patriot Act does not require probable cause (sufficient reason to arrest or search a suspect). Among other things, this means that even without reasonable belief that a crime has been committed, law enforcement officials can freeze assets, tap phones, access private records, and use "sneak and peak" warrants. These warrants allow law enforcement to conduct covert searches of an individual's space. The Patriot Act's new

Freedom Fries

"Freedom Fries" was the name that, for a little while, replaced good old french fries in all restaurants and snack bars run by the House of Representatives. It was part of an attempt by some Republican representatives to garner support for a boycott of French products. The boycott was a response to French criticism of the Iraq invasion in 2003. The language overhaul did not take hold and had little to no effect other than providing fodder for comedians, humorists, and satirists to poke fun at overzealous patriotism.

provisions extend to both U.S. citizens and foreigners living in the United States. In addition, under the Patriot Act, aliens perceived to threaten national security can be held for up to seven days without a formal charge, based solely on reasonable suspicion.

Immediately after the September 11 attacks there was a fierce search for suspected terrorists and supporters all over the world, enabled by the Patriot Act. The joint effort of local and international law enforcement officers eliminated many of the known al-Qaeda cells all over the world. Many of the ringleaders and other terrorists involved in the planning of the attacks were brought to justice. During this time, many Middle Eastern men were deemed suspicious based on little or no evidence other than their Middle Eastern descent.

Public Opinion of the Patriot Act

Public opinion regarding the Patriot Act has undergone quite a transformation since its inception. Based on several Gallup Polls, the Patriot Act enjoyed an almost 50 percent approval rating in January 2002, just after its inception.

Two years later, support for the Act dropped. In November 2003, polls showed only 31 percent of Americans supported the government's curbing of civil liberties under the Patriot Act. Opponents of the Patriot Act claim that it violates the U.S. Constitution.

Another two years later in 2005, polls again suggested approval. This time, the people were again divided almost half and half. However, half the people polled claimed not to know what exactly the Patriot Act entailed.

This was racial profiling. Racial profiling holds an entire group responsible based on the actions of a few. While it is true that the jihadists were Muslim, not all Muslims are jihadists.

Criticism from the voters led to legal action by several state governments, who declared the Patriot Act unconstitutional based on its restrictions of the Bill of Rights. Despite this, it was renewed on March 9, 2006. The debate over the legality of the Act continues.

Are the civil liberties guaranteed by the Bill of Rights untouchable? Are there situations where a government has the right to restrict the rights of its people in order to defend those very rights against outside forces? Is the Patriot Act a move away from the basic U.S. principle that all men are created equal? Does the nation have to allow for racial profiling, or is it persecution?

Opposition to the Patriot Act

Eight U.S. states and some 409 cities and counties have taken legal steps toward nullification of the Patriot Act. Citing the Bill of Rights, they passed resolutions that kept city employees, including police, from assisting any investigation under the Act. Some argue that federal law overrides state and local law, and thus these local resolutions have no validity. The rebuttal, of course, claims that the Constitution overrides federal law. Since the Patriot Act violates some of the Constitution's amendments on civil liberties, it has no validity. In the wake of such massive criticism, some provisions of the Act have been slightly modified.

HOMELAND SECURITY

On October 5, 2001 Thomas Ridge became the first head of the newly created Office of Homeland Security. The Office of Homeland Security provided a context for the Patriot Act. It was part of the overall strategy to prepare the country for potential terrorist attacks. In 2003, based on the Homeland Security Act of 2002, the Office of Homeland Security split into the Department of Homeland Security and the White House Homeland Security Council. The responsibilities of the Department of Homeland Security are threefold:

> *preventing terrorist attacks within the United States, reducing the vulnerability of the United States to terrorism at home, and minimizing the damage and assisting in the recovery from any attacks that may occur.*[1]

To do its job, the Department of Homeland Security fulfills five functions:

> *information analysis and infrastructure protection; chemical, biological, radiological, nuclear, and related countermeasures; border and transportation security; emergency preparedness and response; and coordination with other parts of the federal government, with state and local governments, and with the private sector.*[2]

Tom Ridge is sworn in as the first person to head the new Office of Homeland Security on October 8, 2001.

The Department of Homeland Security oversees 22 formerly self-directed agencies in an effort to protect the United States from terrorism.

The Homeland Security Act is a response to the threat from an unknown and diverse aggressor who operates covertly using modern biological, chemical, and technological weapons. Therefore, the department must be able to easily gather information from various sources, research the weapons used, and prevent aggressors from entering the United States.

On January 8, 2007, New York City Mayor Michael Bloomberg testified before the Senate Homeland Security and Governmental Affairs Committee. He criticized how anti-terror government funds were being distributed and renewed his criticism from 2006. That year, New York and Washington, D.C., the sites of the 9/11 attacks, saw their government grants for terrorism preparedness reduced. Under a formula developed in 2004, 40 percent of the funds are distributed equally among the states, whereas the remaining 60 percent are disbursed depending on population and need based on known threats.

In the few years since it began, the scope and structure of the Department of Homeland Security has been criticized. Many fear that the massive concentration of responsibilities has made the department ineffective, as seen during Hurricane Katrina in August 2005. The Federal Emergency Management Agency (FEMA) and the Department of Homeland Security were criticized over the lack of preparedness as well as the slow and inadequate response to the disaster.

The Department of Homeland Security has also drawn political criticism. By allowing one government office to oversee so many agencies, there is a risk that that power will be abused.

The Homeland Security Act provides that the information gathered on individuals by governmental offices, law enforcement offices, and the private sector must be made accessible to the Department of Homeland Security. In other words, information that was once only available to individual departments or offices can now be collected and consolidated in one single department. Because of this, many worry that private information will become readily accessible to the government and could easily be misused. This renewed concerns over violations of civil liberties allowed through the Patriot Act.

PARTIES DIVIDED

Both the debate over the Patriot Act and the Department of Homeland Security show that despite the unity after the attacks, the country is currently divided on many issues. The Iraq war, for example, was subject of heated debate. It was criticized as unconstitutional because the United States invaded without a formal declaration of war and without the support of a large portion of the U.S. population. President Bush was reelected in 2004 by only a narrow margin, and the campaign showed that the parties were strongly divided.

The 2004 presidential campaign was unusually harsh. The administration used its "with us or against us" viewpoint, casting it against the opposition. The opposition accused the administration of dismantling democracy during discussions of the Patriot Act.

The debates only widened the gap between parties. The use of language to sway public opinion has become subject of debate as well. The phrase "Axis of Evil" placed the War on Terrorism along the lines of good versus evil, evoking an emotional response rather than critical debate.

Similarly, names and acronyms such as "Homeland Security" and "Patriot Act" evoke a sense of patriotism and deem those critical of the policies "un-patriotic." The phrase "War on Terrorism" has been criticized. It suggests military force and does not include or promote other, more peaceful means to fight terrorism. Instead, the term seems to exclude the use of diplomacy, intercultural relations and education, or political and cultural awareness that might encourage an atmosphere of tolerance.

In the years that have passed since the September 11 attacks, the world seems to have moved from the emotional language of "We are all Americans" and "United we stand" to the equally emotional "us against them" and "with us or against us." Neither speech fully describes this complex situation. Is it possible to move beyond either position, and put aside feelings about 9/11, while still paying tribute to its huge emotional toll?

*President George W. Bush delivers a speech asking Congress
for funding to help secure America's borders.*

Albidani   Alyan Al-Wa'eli   Al-Makhlafi   Al-Nahdi   Al-Maktawi   Ammar Al-Wa'eli

Bin Otash   Al-Sabri   Al-Sharari   Al-Hubishi   Al-Sayfi   Al-Ansari

The FBI released photos of 12 suspected terrorists in 2002.

THE 9/11 GENERATION

On October 12, 2002, 202 people died in Bali, Indonesia, as a result of a car bomb planted by a group with al-Qaeda links. On May 12, 2003, 35 people died in Riyadh, Saudi Arabia, when a suicide bomber with suspected al-Qaeda connections attacked three residential compounds. On March 11, 2004, 191 people died in Madrid, Spain, following explosions in commuter trains set off via cell phone by al-Qaeda. On July 7, 2005, 52 people died in London when four suicide bombers with al-Qaeda connections attacked the subway system.

On May 4, 2006, Zacarias Moussaoui, a French citizen of Moroccan descent, was sentenced to life in prison in the United States for his involvement in the 9/11 attacks. The following year, on January 8, 2007, Mounir el-Motassadeq was convicted in Hamburg, Germany, for his involvement in the attacks. He was a member of the Hamburg cell.

Khalid Sheikh Mohammad, the alleged mastermind of the 9/11 attacks, has been in U.S. custody since March 1, 2003. He has been indicted, but as of early 2007, he had not stood trial. Khalid Sheikh Mohammad is also said to have ordered the failed attack on American Airlines 63 by shoe bomber Richard Reid on December 22, 2001. He is also said to have ordered the beheading of journalist

"I don't want to sound Pollyannaish, but I hope that out of a tragedy like this something good will come. I hope we understand we're one family."[1]

—Madeline Albright

Daniel Pearl in February 2002. As of mid-2007, Osama bin Laden was still at large.

LIVING IN A POST-9/11 WORLD

September 11 is not yet over. Perhaps it never will be. The wars in Iraq and Afghanistan are still raging. Death tolls rise steadily. The planned monument at Ground Zero in New York City has not yet been built. Americans have learned what the colors mean on the National Threat Advisory issued on a daily basis by the Department of Homeland Security.

Terrorism seems to have defined the beginning of the new millennium.

September 11 in Arts and Literature

September 11 has been commemorated in art, literature, music, and film. The U.S. postage stamp released on March 2002 showed the firefighters raising the flag on top of the mountain of rubble that once was the World Trade Center. John Adams's 2002 award-winning composition "On the Transmigration of Souls," incorporates information from the missing person signs posted all around New York after the attack.

The 9/11 novel appeared as early as 2003. This new genre includes titles such as Ian McEwan's *Saturday*, Jonathan Safran's *Extremely Loud and Incredibly Close*, and Frederic Beigbeder's *Windows on the World*. *Fahrenheit 9/11*, Michael Moore's critical take on the Bush administration in the aftermath of 9/11 was released in 2004. The 2006 Oliver Stone movie *World Trade Center* focused on the story of two Port Authority Police Officers trapped underneath the rubble.

Will it also define the generation growing up today? Will they live in a culture of fear? Not a fear of an adverse superpower, as in the Cold War, but fear of a "super-empowered individual?"[2] Not a fear of a foreign country, but fear of an individual living next door?

Or will they live in a culture of hope? Hope that the global economy will create global citizens? Hope that education and international communication will be the tools for sincere and lasting intercultural tolerance?

History is always in the making. Governments change their course; public opinion sways. Today, cities, nations, the international community, and humankind are grappling with a singular event of historic proportions.

The ultimate significance of September 11, 2001, will be determined and redetermined for generations to come. Will it be the event that widened the gap between two worlds? Or will it be the event that, even though it came at an unfathomable cost, placed the first

The Colors of the Homeland Security Threat Advisory System

red: severe risk of terrorist attack

orange: high risk of terrorist attack

yellow: significant risk of terrorist attack

blue: general risk of terrorist attacks

green: low risk of terrorist attacks

stone to eventually bridge that gap? It is up to this and future generations to choose. ⌐

"History is the present. That's why every generation writes it anew. But what most people think of as history is its end product, myth."[3]

—E.L. Doctorow

The "Tribute in Light" display honored the victims of September 11.

TIMELINE

1920

British and French rule the Middle East until 1948.

1945

End of World War II. The Cold War begins.

1948

Israel declares independence.

1990

Iraq invades Kuwait. The United States leads UN forces to Saudi Arabia to assist Kuwait. Iraq withdraws February 26, 1991.

1993

A bomb explodes at the World Trade Center, killing six and injuring hundreds February 26.

1997

Osama bin Laden establishes al-Qaeda training camps all over Afghanistan.

September 11, 2001

1979

Ayatollah Khomeini turns Iran into a fundamentalist Islamist state.

1979

Mujahideen from all over the Middle East fight against Soviet occupation. Osama bin Laden helps organize and finance the fight.

1980

Saddam Hussein's Iraq invades Khomeini's Iran. The UN requests that all UN-member states stay out of the conflict.

1998

Mohammad Atta and other 9/11 operatives form the Hamburg cell. Osama bin Laden issues the fatwa.

2001

Mohammad Atta arrives in Madrid, Spain, on July 9 to meet with al-Qaeda operatives and plan the attack.

2001

Terrorists hijack four jetliners and attack the World Trade Center and Pentagon September 11.

TIMELINE

2001	**2001**	**2001**
The last person is found alive in the rubble of the World Trade Center September 12.	Operation Enduring Freedom against the Taliban in Afghanistan begins October 7.	Shoe bomber attack by Richard Reid is thwarted December 22.

2003	**2003**	**2004**
President Bush gives his "Mission Accomplished" speech from aboard the USS *Abraham Lincoln* May 1.	Saddam Hussein is captured December 13.	*60 Minutes II* airs an exclusive on the abuse and torture of prisoners at Abu Ghraib prison in Iraq April 28.

2002

Al Qaeda operatives behead journalist Daniel Pearl. *The National Security Strategy of the United States of America*, also known as the Bush Doctrine, is published.

2003

The Department of Homeland Security is established January 24.

2003

Khalid Sheikh Mohammad is taken into custody March 1. Operation Iraqi Freedom against Iraq begins March 20.

2004

A democratically elected government takes over in Iraq in June. The fighting among guerillas and with the U.S. forces continues.

2004

The 9/11 Commission Report is published in July.

2006

Zacarias Moussaoui is convicted to life in prison due to his involvement in 9/11. Saddam Hussein is convicted of war crimes and sentenced to death.

Essential Facts

Date of Event

September 11, 2001

Place of Event

- ❖ World Trade Center in New York, New York
- ❖ The Pentagon in Arlington, Virginia
- ❖ Shanksville, Pennsylvania

Key Players

- ❖ George W. Bush, United States President
- ❖ Osama bin Laden, al-Qaeda leader
- ❖ Mohammad Atta, al-Qaeda terrorist
- ❖ Rudolph Giuliani, New York City Mayor
- ❖ George Pataki, New York Governor
- ❖ Saddam Hussein, Iraq President

Highlights of Event

❖ Growing Middle Eastern resentment toward the United States following the 1979 war in Afghanistan and the Persian Gulf War.

❖ Osama bin Laden establishes al-Qaeda training camps in 1997.

❖ Members from al-Qaeda's Hamburg cell are recruited for the September 11 attack.

❖ Nineteen hijackers take control of four separate airliners and attack the World Trade Center towers in New York and the Pentagon in Arlington, Virginia.

❖ The United States launches Operation Enduring Freedom against the Taliban government in Afghanistan in retaliation for the attacks.

❖ The United States launches Operation Iraqi Freedom in alignment with a new policy of taking preemptive measures against perceived threats.

❖ Khalid Sheikh Mohammad is taken into custody for his involvement in planning the 9/11 attacks.

❖ Zacarias Moussaoui is imprisoned for his involvement in the 9/11 attacks.

❖ Saddam Hussein is executed on December 30, 2006.

Quote

"A great people has been moved to defend a great nation. Terrorist attacks can shake the foundations of our biggest buildings, but they cannot touch the foundation of America. These acts shattered steel, but they cannot dent the steel of American resolve."—*President George W. Bush*

ADDITIONAL RESOURCES

SELECT BIBLIOGRAPHY

Colombani, Jean-Marie. "We are all Americans," *Le Monde*. Paris, France, September 12, 2001.

Crockatt, Richard. *America Embattled. Anti-Americanism, and the Global Order.* New York: Routledge, 2003.

9/11 Commission. *The 9/11 Commission Report. Authorized Edition.* New York: W.W. Norton & Company, 2004.

Yusufai, Rahimullah. "Wrath of God: Osama bin Laden Lashes Out Against the West." *Time* Magazine. January 11, 1999.

FURTHER READING

Bergen, Peter. *Holy War, Inc.* London: Phoenix Publishers, 2002.

Frank, Mitch. *Understanding September 11*. New York: Viking, 2002.

Hanson, Victor Davis. *An Autumn of War: What America Learned From September 11 And the War On Terrorism.* New York: Anchor Books, 2002.

Lalley, Patrick. *9.11.01 – Terrorists Attack the U.S.* Austin, TX: Steck-Vaughn Company, 2002.

Stewart, Gail. *America Under Attack: September 11, 2001.* Chicago: Lucent Books, 2002.

Wheeler, Jill. *September 11, 2001: The Day That Changed America.* Edina, MN: ABDO Publishing, 2002.

Web Links

To learn more about September 11, visit ABDO Publishing Company on the World Wide Web at **www.abdopublishing.com**. Web sites about September 11 are featured on our Book Links page. These links are routinely monitored and updated to provide the most current information available.

Places to Visit

Ground Zero Museum Workshop
420 West 14th Street
New York, NY 10014
212-209-3370
www.groundzeromuseumworkshop.com
The museum offers photo exhibits documenting the destruction and cleanup of the Twin Towers.

Flight 93 Crash Site Memorial
Shanksville, PA 15560
814-443-4557
www.honorflight93.org
A permanent memorial is being constructed at the crash site of Flight 93 in Shanksville, Pennsylvania. A temporary memorial is in place until then.

Pentagon Memorial
The Pentagon
Washington, D.C. 20050
703-693-8954
http://memorial.pentagon.mil
The memorial park being constructed outside the Pentagon honors the memories of the 184 victims of the Pentagon attack.

GLOSSARY

al-Qaeda

An Arabic word, meaning "the base." The name refers to Osama bin Laden's terrorist organization comprised of militant Muslims and cites religious reasons for its unpredictable and violent attacks on civilians.

anti-Americanism

A set of beliefs and attitudes that is hostile against the government, people, or culture of the United States of America.

Arab

A Middle Eastern person whose first language is Arabic.

capitalism

An economic system in which the means of production are privately owned and governed by supply and demand; the principles of a free market economy.

Cold War

The period between 1945 and 1989, characterized by a standoff between the Soviet Union and the United States.

communism

An ideology pursuing a classless society based on common ownership of the means of production.

fundamentalism

A traditionalist and anti-modernist movement within a religion, requiring strict adherence to the basic principles of the religion.

guerilla

A member of a small independent organization who takes part in irregular fighting against varying opposition.

Islam

A world religion originating with the prophet Muhammed. Prayer and ritual form the pillars of the religion, as much as a sincere belief in sharing and giving to charity as intrinsic goal and value.

Koran
> The central text of Islam which Muslims believe to be the word of God delivered to Muhammed, and therefore indisputable.

monarchy
> A monarchy can have many different forms of government, yet it always has a monarch as head of state.

Muslim
> Followers of Islam.

rogue state
> A state considered a threat to world peace, either by its dictatorial government or is support of terrorism.

sanction
> A measure taken by one nation to coerce another into conforming to international laws.

suicide mission
> A terrorist mission during which the attacker intends to die while taking others with him or her.

Taliban
> A fundamentalist Muslim movement whose militia took control of Afghanistan and has supported al-Qaeda.

terrorism
> Any violent act that targets civilians, meant to spread terror in the name of a cause and not committed by a legitimate government.

Zionism
> The movement for the creation of a national Jewish state in Palestine.

Source Notes

Chapter I. 102 Minutes of Terror

I. George W. Bush. "Statement by the President in his Address to the Nation." The White House. Washington, II Sept. 2001. <http://www.whitehouse.gov/news/releases/ 2001/09/20010911-16.html>.

Chapter 2. A Day in History

I. Maya Angelou. "On the Pulse of Morning." *The Inaugural Poem*. New York: Random House, 1993.

Chapter 3. The Afghanistan Crisis

None.

Chapter 4. U.S. Involvement in the Middle East

I. "Al Qaeda's Fatwa" *News Hour with Jim Lehrer*. PBS. 28 Feb. 1998. Transcript Online News Hour. 19 Mar. 2007. <www.pbs.org/ newshour/terrorism/internatinal/fatwa_1998.html>.

2. Rahimullah Yusufai. "Wrath of God: Osama bin Laden lashes out against the West." *Time* Magazine. Jan. II, 1999. Vol. 153 No. I.

3. "Robert F. Kennedy quotations" *MSN Encarta,* Seattle: Microsoft, 2007. 19 Mar. 2007. <http://encarta.msn.com/refedlist_210046598_3/ Fanaticism_What_is_objectionable_what_is.html>.

Chapter 5. Anti-American Sentiments

None.

Chapter 6. The Origins of Jihad

1. "UN Reform." *UNifeed.* Web Services Section Department of Public Information. New York: United Nations, 2005. 19 Mar. 2007. <http://www.un.org/unifeed/script.asp?scriptId=73>.

2. George W. Bush. "Backgrounder: The President's Quotes on Islam." The White House, Washington, Nov. 13, 2002. 19 Mar. 2007 <http://www.whitehouse.gov/infocus/ramadan/islam.html>.

3. George W. Bush. "Address to a Joint Session of Congress and the American People." The White House. Washington, 20 Sept. 2001. 19 Mar. 2007. <www.whitehouse.gov/news/releases/2001/09/20010920-8.html>.

4. United Nations. "Article 3." *Universal Declaration of Human Rights.* New York: Taylor, 1948. <www.un.org/Overview/rights.html>.

Chapter 7. We Are All Americans

1. NATO. "Article 5." *The North Atlantic Treaty.* Washington: GPO, 1949. 19 Mar. 2007 <www.nato.int/docu/basictxt/treaty.htm>.

2. "International Reaction: In their own words." *September 11 News.com.* 2003. 19 Mar. 2007. <http://www.september11news.com/InternationalReaction.htm>.

Chapter 8. International Issues

1. George W. Bush. "Statement by the President in his Address to the Nation." The White House. Washington, 11 Sept. 2001, 19 Mar. 2007 <http://www.whitehouse.gov/news/releases/2001/09/20010911-16.html>.

2. Ibid.

3. George W. Bush. "Address to a Joint Session of Congress and the American People." The White House. Washington, 20 Sept. 2001. 19 Mar. 2007. <www.whitehouse.gov/news/releases/2001/09/20010920-8.html>.

Source Notes Continued

Chapter 9. Domestic Issues

1. United States. White House. *Analysis for the Homeland Security Act of 2002.* Section 101. Washington: GPO, 2002. 19 Mar. 2007 <http://www.whitehouse.gov/deptofhomeland/analysis/hsl-bill-analysis.pdf>.

2. Ibid.

Chapter 10. The 9/11 Generation

1. Madeline Albright. Interview with Oprah Winfrey. "Making Sense of The Unimaginable," *O Magazine.* Dec. 2001.

2. Thomas L Friedman. "The Super-Empowered Angry Man." *The Lexus and the Olive Tree.* New York: Random House, 2001.

3. E. L. Doctorow. *Billy Bathgate.* New York: Plume, 1998.

INDEX

ABOUT THE AUTHOR

Helga Schier holds a Ph.D. in language and literature. She writes and edits with a compassion for history, a love of the present, and excitement for the future. She lived in New York City for many years before she moved to Santa Monica, California with her husband and two children.

PHOTO CREDITS

Ron Haviv/AP Images, cover, 3; Chao Soi Cheong/AP Images, 6, 97 (bottom); John Labriola/AP Images, 11; Lindaanne Donohoe, 13, 29; James Nachtwey/AP Images, 15, 16, 98 (top); Stephen J. Boitano/AP Images, 21; Bob Martin/AP Images, 22, 97 (top); Ricardo Mazalan/AP Images, 30, 96 (top); Bill Haber/AP Images, 37; AP Images, 41, 58, 96 (bottom); Fabian Bimmer/AP Images, 42; Heribert Proepper/AP Images, 47; Christopher Morris/AP Images, 50; B.K. Bangash/AP Images, 53; Lee Celano/AP Images, 54; Alexandra Boulat/AP Images, 63, 71; Gulnara Samoilova/AP Images, 64; Mike Segar, Pool/AP Images, 69; Ryan O'Connor/MOD/Pool/AP Images, 72; Scott Nelson/Pool/AP Images, 79, 99 (bottom); Susan Walsh/AP Images, 80; J. Scott Applewhite/AP Images, 85, 89, 98 (bottom), 99 (top); FBI/AP Images, 90; Bela Szandelsky/AP Images, 95.